After the Vows

Poems Between Lovers

David M Pitchford
Siobhan M Pitchford

Published by
Diminuendo Press
Imprint of Cyberwizard Productions
1205 N. Saginaw Boulevard #D
PMB 224
Saginaw, Texas 76179

Edited by Crystalwizard

Cover Artist: A.R. Stone

After the Vows:
Poems Between Lovers
Copyright © 2008 Cyberwizard Productions
Individual poems copyright © 2008 David M Pitchford &
Siobhan M Pitchford
ISBN: 978-0-9815669-3-1 (paper)
ISBN: 978-0-9815669-4-8 (electronic)
Library of Congress Control Number: 2008927712
First Edition:

Siobhan is my wife, my muse, my lover, and, most importantly, my friend. We met via poetry on an internet forum. It doesn't matter how long ago; we've had the best fifty-year marriage I can imagine, and it's taken less than decade... This project was spawned both by our incessant need to articulate ourselves to each other, and by a complementary competitive spirit. We drive each other to excel. I certainly hope there is plenty of evidence throughout this collection. And, though it seems the strangest thing to me, I hope you, our readers, find good examples within these sonnets. Sio and I both learned how to swim the deep waters by choking on the brine, as it were. What they don't tell us in school is that this thing called "commitment" is not something you do once and have done with it. Commitment is a long-term endeavor; each day, each temptation, each new situation is a chance to renew commitment. To do otherwise is not commitment. It was a long and arduous road for me to this knowledge; I hope to mark a clearer trail for anyone on the same journey. Yes, marriage is about love. It's about sex. It's about joy and fun and honeymoons. And it's also about stubbing your toe at midnight on a nightstand your spouse moved for no particular reason; it's about growing apart, and then learning to come back together; it's about living your own life with a roadie, and about being a roadie for another's life; it's about waking up next to a person more familiar to you than yourself and realizing that you're someone you don't recognize; it's about forgiveness and perseverance. And every romantic relationship should be all those things as well. Poetry is life's soundtrack—sometimes a love song, others a dirge. Enjoy our soundtrack; may it enrich your life and spark your own passion for life!

David M Pitchford
April 2008

Poetry is my lifeline; it is what makes me truly alive. It is also extremely personal and intimate, which makes writing an introduction to this collection a challenge. The poetry contained in this slim volume, for it is slim in relation to the number of sonnets David and I have written to one another since our marriage in 1999, is a glimpse into our lives. As they are about life as it is, some of them are sensual, sexy even. Just as life has such moments. Scattered among these are poems about everyday things—enjoying lunch together, listening to one another drone on about the workday, even dragging ourselves out of bed to exercise. Still others deal with the fear of being unworthy of love or 'not enough' for our partner; the attempt to handle being alone versus feeling alone in a relationship; and working through the anger as well as the sadness, the sickness and the health we spoke in our vows. These poems capture the words we need to say after we've said "I do", the actions we need to remember to remain lovers no matter how long we're together, and the intimacy we all long for in whatever relationship we happen to enter into. I hope you enjoy these glimpses. I hope you can learn from them as much as we do. And, most of all, I hope they enrich your life as they have ours.

Live well, laugh often, love much.
Siobhan M Pitchford
April 2008

TABLE OF CONTENTS

HYMN TO HER

I long to be Orpheus when it comes
to you; to sing and play with grace enough
to swell your heart forever. I love you,
truly, but most days are merely days, and
I find my tongue tied up in mundane words
powerless to reflect my condition
in relation to you. I'm affected,
yes, but not like in school days, neither
in boyish ways, but as a man, and with
a sturdiness of earth, with seasons, some
brighter, some dim—Oh, to be Orpheus
and sing you such love and with such spirit
that even celestial beings sigh
for having heard our mortal passions play.

Aphrodite in your shadow

So well you take me as I am. I fear
to imagine what would be should that fair-
fortuned force that fogs your eyes suddenly
shed the scales that put me in your vision
as you describe it. I see no such man
within my mirror, but thank the heavens
that you see me so. And how do I see
you? Aphrodite shone as bright, I'm sure,
yet your steadfast nature is earth scented,
unlike Venus's too fickle fragrances,
therefore so much the more desirable.
Yet, how can I compare you and be fair
when she is myth and you of fleshly make
she I wonder of—you I worldly hold.

you are not orpheus

You are not Orpheus, love, nor would I
have you be, and I will not slip in to
Hades hands. Understand my love is new
even when mundane is the order of
the day and I wish for words of passion
and wit. My days are incomplete without
a kiss from your lips, in a smile or pout.
Fanciful dreams in romantic fashion
still find their way into the world around
me, but now my prince has a face I can see
and when I look in your eyes, I see me.
My name in your voice is sweeter, I say
more musical than any poetry,
or song, Orpheus ever thought to play.

BESIDE ME IN THE DARKNESS

Cradled in the sigh of gods and goddess
we run through this life accepting moments—
gifts of time when the world is only us.
Laughter and passion share space with sadness
and quiet, wrapping us closer into
each other. Most days my sun shines brightly
and at night, the moon is more poetic
than mere mortals often see. It is you
that makes it so. You lay beside me in
darkness, my light, the completion of me.
Your touch, new and different, sparks long dormant
thoughts and feelings I want to believe in.
Your whispers answer my own, your dreams blend
with mine. We are separate and together.

who you are

Yesterday I watched you play with our boys
in the sun filled afternoon, with laughter
light on your tongue and face. I knew again
I'd found my place in a world that has not
always been easy—for any of us.
I long to give you more than you say you
need—or want. I wish to be the woman
of your dreams, yet real enough to hold you
in this world. Whether muse or forgotten
whimsy takes hold of your passionate mood
I wish that it was me inspiring you,
and you could see what I do when looking—
not Adonis or Dionysus or
any other god—just the man I love.

By your side

You are right to say I am no godling.
No, I never was pretty enough to
be Adonis, and what is more, though quite
adept at taking such joy as wine gives,
never led others into my madness,
so let Dionysus also keep his
name. Yes, love, only you can bring this
mortal's fame to any kind of honor,
though reputation really is a thing
a man can grow beyond, unlike your love—
and what man with any sense ever would
wish to wander from it; sooner would earth
decide to shun the moon. It's by your side
I stand, there belong for life or longer.

SWEET ELIXIR

You are as handsome as midnight moonlight
on my rose garden, mystical and dark.
I get drunk on the mystery of you.
Your kisses are more potent than any
wine you pour, your touch is flame that lights fire
within this imperfect body of mine.
I, too, am adept in many things, yet
will always welcome the chance to learn from
you what ignites the man within. Our life
a precious gift to me, a private love
for us to share, discover and explore—
our bodies together, a place of sweet
surrender. My love for you goes beyond
words to dreams unspoken and hope renewed.

WE: YOU AND ME

We sip wine from overflowing cups, and
you speak of midnight and moonlight as we
dance to wine's sweet red rhythm and spare soft
sighs for past years we went unknown to each
other, becoming each who we are to
become the we of you and me. I think
stars never shone so bright as when I learned
to see them through your eyes. No other voice
brought such sweetness clinging to lines of verse
till yours taught my ears more than longing, and
so soon my heart followed in contentment.
I dream no dream now, but live this life with
you, to dream no more till the black softness
that is death closes my eyes forever.

The we of you and me

I would have you speak of dreams, not your death
in the same breath as celebrates our love.
With you, I am learning yesterday is
behind me—although when alone, it creeps
in, and I find myself longing for you—
your arms about me and your lips on mine.
You taught me to see today, instead of
leaping into tomorrow. The future
holds out its hands and beckons me—come
dance into this light. And I turn to you
knowing the path I walk is by your side.
The me that was alone no longer dreams
of places far away. My heart and home
are found within the we of you and me.

the bRiDGe thAt spANs time

That you speak of hailing tomorrow
is fit, and I should write of yesterdays'
glories. You look ahead so oft, and I
look back as much. Could this equation be
time's reason for standing still as we dance
together? I am certain of it. Love
must surely be the bridge that spans time's swift
channel. And so it is that lovers stand
above these currents when enraptured. And
so it is that when together we stand
within the moment, outside of time, and
somehow above mortality. So now,
hold me, forget all existence beyond
this one particular moment of now.

THE MOMENT OF NOW

Each time I hold you, love, I am newly
amazed that this present moment can be—
is—more precious than any one before.
The wonder of you and me is beyond
comparison and so do I dismiss
yesterday, except for hard-learned lessons.
They bear remembering, not repeating.
The steps of this dance are ours together.
When future fears sweep me to deep water,
I reach for you and know you will hold me.
When you look to drown in your past, my arms
are here, love, to hold you in our moment.
Hear music dance in rhythm with these lines
written to express how I feel for you.

IN MELANCHOLY'S SHADOW

Days when you are gone to work, I sometimes
sit in melancholy's shadow and brood
for things I cannot name. So many times,
the day passes so slowly, yet nothing
gets done. Those times, it is as if I were
adrift with no wind to fill these slack sails
and push this ship to shores that once welcomed
who I thought was me. At times this darkness
closes about me far too close, chains me
in some inner prison where I fear I'll
never again see day's glorious light.
But then you come home, greet me with a kiss
and gaze that warms more thoroughly
than Helios in his faraway sky.

iMpRiSONED

You are not alone in your prison or
melancholy's shadow for she follows
me to work on grey days when I wish to
remain in bed, tangled in sheets with you.
Work passes across my desk and I sit,
unable to focus, wanting your call,
to hear you've not forgotten I exist.
I become impatient for word from you.
My mind plays tricks with time and I reel back
into the past I have sworn to dismiss.
I wonder if I am enough to keep
you in this moment, with me and our life.
I write words of desire you may not read
to remind myself that your love is real.

effortless, peaceful hours

Other days, it seems you never leave, though
in body, you're off to work. Those times, all
day I write or work around our house and
each moment anticipate your greeting
from the other room. Chores seem to complete
themselves with assertion of only will.
Effortless, peaceful hours pass by with
my fingertips flying over keyboard
in ten–thousand clicks, and like magic these
words appear upon the screen decrying
passions I'd near forgotten I possess.
Well you taught me that I indeed own them,
and their days of owning me are past with
my adolescence, and youth's awkwardness.

ON THOSE DAYS

When I leave the house, you sleeping soundly
in our bed, and the kitchen is a mess,
and the children have been fussy, I rail
at you in my head. I rant and I rave,
for you to take away the strain of it.
And then, when sitting up to my elbows
in projects, you call—my frustration melts.
Tears form and dribble down unpainted cheeks,
and I smile. I can hear in your tone love
for me and how much you miss having me
with you—knowing my spirit always is
even when my body is miles away.
I have grown with you and the love you give
beyond the starry-eyed girl I once was.

if you go

You seem sometimes to misinterpret my
soft grip as being loose as if I would
let you go for no good reason, or worse,
that I hold you away to let my heart
or eyes or wonder roam. This lesson was
hard for me to learn: commitment wears no
shackles, he who holds to keep will longer
hold than he whose holding fears to lose. When
it seems I've let you go, it merely is
because I know you'll stay here at my side;
and if you go, I know it's only to
return. So next time you think that I have
strayed, look closer to yourself. It may be
I've withdrawn more into you than away.

Losing Fear

Fear of losing you—or losing me—sits
inside and hides. This, my weakness, does not
show itself as often as it used to,
perhaps its hold has lessened since we met.
When I wonder if you long to wander
away from me, I look at what you see
and I realize that above all else
I can be found when I look in your eyes.
It has taken me time and your patience
to bring me to the place where I can let
go of you and know in my heart we are
always connected; that your home and heart
are here with me. And so, love, no longer
do I fear your cave—it is found in me.

DOWN LINES WE CANNOT TRACE

Nine muses came down the Olympian
lines, sprang from Mnemosyne's loins, fathered
by Prometheus, though most say Zeus. And so,
somehow, down lines we cannot trace, came their
soft, strange power to you. Lines you pen speak
of timeless passions, wondrous scenes you paint
bring forward ancient glories danced by elves
in glens, pirouettes you dance throughout our
house speak joy your heart cannot selfish hide,
and surely trouble you borrow is learned
from tragic twists you have witnessed throughout
history—lived down the long turns of time's
great vortex, each reincarnation one
more spin on the sky's ever-turning wheel.

ANCIENT LOVE

My lines are old, ancient as this passion
I have for you. It was just yesterday
I followed you out of Hades and slipped
back just as quickly at your glance. You've learned,
as have I, from the adventures of our
ancestors that this love belongs to the
moment in which we live. My pen speaks of
passion's shared chant. My dance celebrates us,
our life is the reincarnation of
all great loves through history. My path has
twisted and left me scars that I thought would
never heal. You brought me joy and a love
I dare to speak and share. It is with you
I look to somehow make my muses proud.

WITH YOU, SILENT COMFORT

Mortality feels an unbearable
infection some days. Its only cure is
death. Aside from that, it has one relief,
and that is love. In this life you wear its
mantle; you nurse me, keep my pain somehow
lessened to the point my howling ceases.
With you, silent comfort sometimes visits.
At moments, and only in your presence,
I feel our common disease slough off to
leave us in eternity's lush embrace
of warmth and wholeness. How cold it seems in
moments between, when we each go to times
of solitary dream within spaces
of our sweet enduring togetherness.

SONNET IN JANUARY

Treading lightly in the wake of some dream
I walk about in this world more aware
of people passing by me, how they stare
at our passion, as if to them we seem
lost in a now far away from here where
they are wrapped in the tangible group mess
called life. Our indifference may seem less
than generous to the place they all share,
but in our world we celebrate and bless
the joy of living. We remember each
moment of being and when lonely, reach
for one another, hold close and confess
deep secrets in whispers meant for our ears
alone. We laugh and love away the years.

PARADISE ONCE REMOVED

Yes. To laugh and to love the years away
in full lives and days spent in embraces
where night's kiss lingers heavy on your lids,
eyes wanting never to open if it
means parting from hugs warm as Spring's first sun
after long, winter-cold nights that linger
beyond thresholds. We rub noses between
kisses—nuzzles for us to learn again
each other's aura, energized again
like the new morning's sun that shines through
our window, reminiscent of those first
sunrises we shared together—ones where
paradise was wherever we shared each
other's breath, embraced within heaven's reach.

LONG MORNING HOURS

Long morning hours drag past, slow motion
movement, I drift in and out of focus.
Piles of work sit around, an ocean
of the mundane, waiting for attention.
I do not give it more than a passing
glance, for you fill my mind, invading all
I do. Each little thought tugs at my sleeve
asking for more. Had I the means, I would
whisk you away with me, to temperate
climates, where we two would write and read and
love the hours together. Yes, we would
explore, invent, create, and be, my love.
Morning hours would no longer drag on.
Days would be too short, nights not long enough.

The Ship That Sails Me

Morning oceans of mundane? Forgive me
my optimism, but you are the ship
that sails me out on seas of dream. Long nights
and days that pass landlocked leave a sailor
dry beyond his wont. Longing and sea-swells
all he knows worth living for, and harbors
where the fair of each new land greet warmly
their roving souls. That life was mine, and full
until the port wherein we met. Those eyes
stole this sailor from the sea. Better now,
my life is fuller of you than ever
it was the sea. How I treasure your love
and this port by far the richest to call,
though any we could call home—or all.

WONDERING WHERE YOU ARE

When I find myself sitting, staring at
a blinking screen all covered with letters,
I realize my mind has drifted to
wonder where you are. I have not yet heard
from you, in sweet-keyed message or husky
voiced voice mail and I miss you. It does not
get easier, giving of space and time
to do what you need to do—yet I can
and will. When I need beyond endurance
I write words you may read or maybe not.
I know the distance between us, love, is
only as far as our thoughts. Still I ask—
Do you think of me, or wonder just where
I am in the hours when I am gone?

COMFORTABLE ENOUGH

My trust of you holds no room for doubt. When
you are later than I think you should be,
I seldom fret about you. Though, truth is,
sometimes my mind creates scenarios
in which your circumstances outweigh your
control, and my dark imagination
takes hold to hint at disasters that may
have befallen you somewhere between the
place you should be and where you are. But then
I remind myself that you can hold your
own, and that this time would be better served
in preparation for your return
than in worthless worry. So, then I smile,
comfortable enough to wait for a while.

COMFORTABLE

I wake in the early light, casting dreams
aside at the buzzing of the alarm,
you reach out, hold me in the curl of your
body, sharing your warmth. I imagine
what it would be like to roll over,
stay with you. For the briefest moment I
do before carefully shrugging out from
beneath our blankets. Freshly showered, I
return to you, sliding the towel from
my shoulders, I offer you my back for
lotion—our morning ritual, relish
the feel of your hands sliding across me.
I leave a breakfast of grapefruit and love
poems for you, smiling into the day.

CATCH MY ATTENTION

What would lunch be without us together?
Especially on days you've left me gifts,
knowing I might sleep for hours after
you've gone to work. For example, take this
morning: you left me grapefruit, cut for me
so that I would have the most convenience
you could leave for me. You left it at the
table's head, just behind a small vase of
carnations you'd arranged from a larger
bouquet. You left me the freshest, perky
reds and sexy white ones with the pink fringe.
Even your poems, there for me to read.
Believe me, these things catch my attention
and keep me in mind of your affection.

CApCURiNG YOUR ACCENCiON

Small notes to be found whenever you least
expect them, a bar of chocolate, or
a single flower—is simpler some days
than finding the words—or the poetry—
to tell you how I feel. Days come and go
when I see you leave me for a moment—
lost in thoughts I cannot follow. These times
bring me to the edge of wanting to reach
out and pull you close. But I can't intrude
so I leave the gift to remind you, to
capture your attention and let you know
I am here—willing to share the simple
pleasures of being together with you,
whenever you want to be with me, love.

PERFECT MOMENTS

It could have been a French Bistro, and our
faithful Steiner the maitre d'. One lush
tomato, two luscious steaks flavored with
pepper and brandy, and potatoes mashed
with garlic. (Too bad lunch must cry for wine
and hear no answer.) We two made for a
friendly crowd unto ourselves. Another
perfect moment of Now—a few kisses
washed down with filtered water—oh, did I
mention missing the wine?—parting words in
a language only you and I know. The
roughness of my hands cause crackles like spark
sounds as I slide them down your wool pants. A
promised future—parting, we wave kisses.

GARLiC kiss

The taste of garlic mingles in our kiss
and you smile a laugh in my direction.
Who needs wine for such simple pleasures as
we share, love? Not me. I relish the taste
of you, the way you look at me across
the table—breakfast, lunch, or late supper,
by candlelight or moon, day's full sunshine
it matters not to me as long as you
and I share the time. Electricity
jumps between us, arching across the space
igniting the passion that curls below
the surface whenever you are near me.
Your hands slide along wool while I wrap my
arms around you for one more garlic kiss.

WHAT WE MOST TREASURE

What is a flaw but a mark of human
character? Does it not show the man or
woman mortal whose perfection is more
coarse than the ideal we so pretend to
honor above all? What is the worth of
perfection? Perfection needs for nothing,
and so how can any need it? Complete
unto itself? Then it is inhuman,
and therefore of no value to us. Are
we not human? Have we not our own flaws
to show to the world our true character?
This between us is what we most treasure
about each other. Character and flaws.

Loving Every Flaw

You laud your laurels and brandish them well
the words your pen and ink dip to paper,
and so you should for words are your caper
across, and through, this life you say is hell
on days and nights when dreams haunt but don't tell
you what they mean or want, being just vapor
in the evening breeze. You sit by taper
light, wax dripping to table top, in spell-
bound trance scratching the surface of your dreams,
writing all life's memories as they fall
from your mind to paper. I watch in awe;
your passage into this other world seems
to whisk you away from me. I feel all
at once, part of you, loving every flaw.

Love in Time

How long can passion burn star-like in the
night sky? Does it sometimes dim in the full
moon's boisterous glow, and in Luna's dark
shine brighter still? Do eyes sometimes brighten
late at night, as well as early in morn?
What time in life does passion burn hottest?
Youth has spent us—sent us on to kinder
decades. We embrace now more decadent
for having longer passion that burns cool
more than tedious youth allowed. Thank God
and all the high heavenly hosts above
for this seemly glimpse of a love that might
beat out temporal probability
to shine brightly throughout Eternity.

whispering

Whispering in the world's loud, hurried sound
is a message for you and me, ageless
as time. "I love you" vibrations echo
across the moments that separate us.
I delight in the feel—your memory,
draping me in a cloak of fairie dust.
Ethereal sensations, fantasy
I know to be reality—you, me
growing in fractions, closer together.
No longer needing the reassurance
of new lovers—yet still holding the same
passion for one another as when new.
The murmur of your voice fills my dreaming,
I hear the words you whisper in the noise.

time thief

A kiss. A hug. Time spent. Time owed. We two.
Well-spent time in a hug with you, and time
means nothing next to kisses sweet as my
lover's lips on mine. Oh! How she holds me!
Moments seem forever with her—longer
away! What lips but hers can fit kisses
for me? None, I swear it! Time's such a thief
of love! Dastard of dastards, to steal my
love's short time from me, and mine from she who
worships me with her embrace, her sweet face,
and fair words blown to my ear from spaces
made meaningless by love. Were we to rob
time as meanly as he robs us, surely
Eternity's kisses would seal our love.

SUNRISE, SUNSET

Whether at sunrise or sunset or all
the hours in between, with you is where
I belong. Even when we are apart,
love, hold a piece of me inside of you.
Carry me along through your daily chores
into your books and studies, fantasies
and dreams. Play with the memory of our
most recent kisses—surely not the last—
and think on how it feels to hold me close,
my touch along your cheek and lips so sweet.
And when you find yourself drifting off in
daydreams of when next we'll be together
remember I, too, am thinking of time
spent together—sunrises and sunsets.

BOUNDLESS

Funny how life can seem to start later
for some than others. I don't think my life
began until I met you . . . NO, Strike that!
That would be too unfair for those whose hearts I
climbed to reach your tower. I would rather
honor them, and, really, I have a lot
of affection for them still. But surely,
anyone with eyes can see my passion
holds only you for target now. Maybe
years are stacking up. Funny now, how young
thirty-something seems from this vantage point.
But there's plenty more hill in front of us,
too soon now to think of stopping. Let's go
together beyond every known boundary.

SCENT OF LOVE

This faint grey in my mane is softer than
the steel caressing the frame of your face.
You are older than the calendar does
declare, and more full of life than most men.
It is your spirit and the depth of you
I have known across millennia past.
And it is this you I find anew, love,
each day I wake in our marriage bed.
At morning light, when I slip from between
warm sheets, your scent clings to me, a silken
reminder of our love made in the dark
surrounded by the house we've made a home.
I am loath to wash your scent away, love,
even knowing love's scent will come again.

UNTIL MORNING

Darkness whispers late at night. It lies of
times we had no knowledge of each other—
times we both spent nights alone and lonely,
searching for what could only find us if
we let it alone. I listen to you
softly breathe, and the darkness seems lighter,
weighs less on this soul of mine that never
seemed to quite outlive those lonely nights, though
they hold only ghostly shapes of bitter
dreams or sinister memory, tainted
emotion. Upon waking, I feel the
very real warmth of your flesh beneath my
palm, and roll over once again to live
in peaceful slumber until morning comes.

Late at Night

Late at night, when whispers in the darkness
are mine to hear alone, I look at you
sleeping, and marvel that at one time I
knew nothing of the man who put this spark
back into my life. All my hopes and dreams
had faded in everyday apathy,
symptoms of emotion's sad absence;
of living this life just to get by.
Now passions rumble their bright vibrations
through my daily chores. Even when alone,
I feel your thoughts of me echo across
town, finding a spot to settle inside
me. I've shaken off the dust of old loves
and revel in my days and nights with you.

OF A MORNING

I feel you move early in the morning
and know of your hesitation to break
the silence of a well-rested night. I
sense apathy's bite on your heart and dive
for the colors of vivid dream, grasping
at your hand, wishing to pull you down with
me into frolics we enjoy within
that fairer realm. Sometimes it is bliss to
hold you there. But other times you refuse
to come along. I know you'd rather join
me in the quicksilver waters beneath
the falls, among the taunting voices of
invisible folk, but today you don
propriety's attire, and leave me to dream.

EARLY MORNING LIGHT

Dust dances through early light whispering
between the curtains. Winter's cold fingers
creep along the edge of our blanketed
bodies, curled around one another.
I waken in fractions, so unwilling
to leave dreams of warm-breezed sandy beaches
where we run along the brink of the world
heaven separated from earth by sea.
Apathy, a rare emotion in me,
sends vibrations of indifference through
our room as the bedside alarm shatters
the silence and I turn it off—again.
One more minute is all I ask—for time
to stand still long enough for me to dream.

A Thought Away

Separation anxiety takes such
a toll on you sometimes. How can I ease
the pain? What magic words will take the cold
knife of isolation from that pretty
throat of yours? Doesn't absence make the heart
grow fonder? It's no excuse to wander,
but to console you. I hold great value
in your security, emotional
as much as physical. I'm still as close
as a thought away, even when you are
out of arms' reach, and I am unable
to hold you, and to push away the cold.
Content you in the knowledge that my heart
is filled with you, and I will hold you soon.

hold me

Exquisite pain, not ecstasy at all
just that ache of missing you that builds up
inside me when I know we'll be apart
for longer than I want to imagine.
Imagination is my enemy
when we are separated by space and
the time it takes to get to you stretches
far across daylight and into evening.
Thoughts entangled in memories play tricks
on me. I misplace the moment I know
with visions of chance encounters where you
walk by me and, not knowing who I am,
forget to smile and stop me with a kiss.
Help me to banish this pain, love—hold me.

The Color of Our Eyes

Overcast Aphrodite, the color
of your eyes, like seafoam under silver
clouds, where languid waves roll the ocean from
moon to exotic shores where we frolic
together under heaven's broad blanket
and love through timeless moments, where cherubs
and muses serenade us, and dance to
flute and drum, strings and brass, bells and every
sweet melody conceived for human joy—
where sweetest flowers ever bloom for me
to pluck and gift you in living vases,
or braid within your flowing flaxen locks.
Are my eyes as blue as the deep, drenching
melancholy that holds us when apart?

By you

Ocean blue grey awash with mist, clouded
with memory, appears to spill over
in clear water falls—dreams of the rover
you once were remain around you, shrouded
within the moment of now, where we live
in ways we never thought we ever would
nor dreamt outside poetry even could.
Allow the grey green of my eyes to give
you the breath of life you have given me.
Take the spark of life buried here inside
this body of mine, share your life, decide
to step out of the cave, look around and see
the dreams and reality inspired
in this woman who would be desired.

SUBTEXT TO EVERY LINE

So much is false that finds its way into
the human heart, but I try fervently
throughout my life to keep myself and my
dealings genuine. It has always been
easy with you—to be genuine, though
at times my strange bravado seems shallow
deception to cover tender chinks in
my self-esteem's soft armor. I ever
attain to bravery in your arms, and
by your side remain stalwart. I never
want sympathy, nor anything less than
love from you. Truth, beauty, and passion is
our credo. "I love you" is the subtext
to every line we speak to each other.

ÐUST

I would have felt no sympathy for you,
love, had you been like so many before
who whispered and laughed at my ramblings
while feigning interest. You threw apathy
across the room, in my direction, and
I knew it to be false—a shell cover
masking symptoms of our impending
love begun with lust. I would be less than
honest if I said I did not delight
in the vibrations of your gaze reaching
across my consciousness, leaving the dust
of your image in my mind, setting it
deep inside my heart. I hear your message
in fractions of speech saying you love me.

FEELING SILLY

I imagine you at work, half-a-mile
away, and wonder if you are thinking
of me, maybe with a faint blush to your
cheeks, and the distinct glow of a woman
in love. My smile feels so silly at such
times, but these moments it is good to feel
silly. For all that I'm worth, I don't mind
being the butt of schoolboy jokes if it
means I'm the one who takes you home tonight.
Sympathy for others never occurs
when I think of what we'll do together
under Night's brazen blanket. All the world
can pass into obscure dissolution for
all I care. But we are for Evermore!

i Think of you

Sitting at my desk I can look out the
window and just barely see the top of
where you are. I imagine you inside
a building of non-descript color, you
working alongside people you have just
met and I wonder if they see in you
the qualities that I love. My thoughts wander
to this morning, seeing you step out from
the shower, ready yourself for the day.
I feel the memories run through me, chase
each other to my core. I long for you,
the moment I will walk into your arms,
fall into our bed—give you, show you this
passion sweet and never ordinary.

CREMBLE

Absorbing the negative energy
flowing from you, pulling it to a place
inside me—I work to provide the space
in our world for your peace, a synergy
of my love for you—and of yours for me.
It pains me to see the anguish your face
displays when darkness descends, sadness laced
dreams invade and your eyes no longer see
the wonders around you. Lost to all of
us, you withdraw inside, silent voices
whisper in your ear, drag happiness from
within your grasp, deny any could love
such a man. I tremble at the choices
of how to bring you back—no longer numb.

ShARiNG

Knots I'm tied in only time unravels,
but you my love make brighter the dimness
of days I view from this prison within.
Such nights no stars shine through, and fickle Moon
withholds her loveliness from me alone—
your smile is my heart's illumination
through such bitter malaise, and your voice soothes
what no words or superstitions may. Life
is void then, but your presence is promise
that better days dawn down Time's slow river
where we again can be together in
fields of beauty, under azure skies.
Does it comfort you to be my comfort?
Can we share this—and not my agony?

PASSION FOR LOVE

I close my ears until I hear your words
"I love you" following me into dream.
Inside that secret sanctum I can cry
and plead with you to talk to me of love,
forget outside world terror, approaching
peril, the nay-sayers of peace-on-earth.
But when I wake, it returns, surrounds me
clamoring from radio and TV
interrupted only by blazing fire
or winter's blizzard news—never any
pleasant diversions to carry us off
away from war and a world gone to hell.
Can we end this rhetoric of horror?
Return, instead, to a passion for love?

iNTiMATe NiGhT

Silver-lined eyes of green, flecked with gold stare
into these—velvet salvation comes in
the intimate night of lovers/friends. Full
moon over dark mountains entwined beneath
star-bathed escarpments. Peace is the sliver
music heard within ears whose mystery
allows all love rumors, yet disavows
lies of war—this is soft revolution
passive! Disenfranchised—bold Aggression
is the tea warmongers drink in summer
sunsets. Dissidents move through winter's end
to disperse imagination's despots
un-united figures stand in shadows'
disarray. Salvation in full armor.

WHAT CAN'T BE SEEN

By starlight the single face of lovers
kissing becomes one vision—seldom two.
Against green grass carpets beneath a tree
bodies entwined blend into one being.
Seeing what can't be seen, playing eye-tricks
with images, bringing fantasy to
everyday life—inspiring through words
worlds of passion, happiness, love and lust.
Beyond what's really there, and what we want,
lies possibilities brave souls dream—think—
write about. Lines of prose and poetry
meant for one and all—only you and me.
What can't be seen inside these words is you,
moonlight, stars, rainy days, and nights alone.

This sensuous blossom

How many times can the same love blossom?
Should the warm sun of kindness continue
to shine upon it through bright, tender eyes
and words of beauty drop down to drench it,
or merely bejewel it like cool dew
each morning over recalled vivid dreams
and coffee kisses through every season
often crowned in brilliant moonlight waxing
and waning to dark for brief respite now
and then, cooled in heated days by mild winds
of affirmation and adoration
spoken in low tones by beloved's voice
and seen in every gentle action, or
felt in every glancing kiss of soft lips.

TORN APART

I came across pages of poetry
you wrote when swallowed by another's love.
You were consumed by thoughts, feelings for her.
And I wondered when the ripping feelings
inside of me would fade; the sensation
of being torn apart slowly when I
hear the words penned for another lover,
a woman who held all your affections
tightly in her grasp, before you and I
knew we even existed. And I scream
silently for you to stop reading them,
stop writing them, stop remembering her.
Jealousy does not become me, so I
listen for our love in your words before.

Looking Back, Living Now

You are right to say that jealousy un-
becomes you. It's strange that fear of losing
something can drive us to throw it away—
that is the one fault I hate most about
human nature. You handle it better
than you think you do, and much better than
most I have known. There speaks our problem—
the others I've known. I've been where I've been,
done what I've done, and known whom I've known, and
there's no going back to undo done deeds.
It's a matter of trust—I'm still here,
I made promises, and several years
now kept them faithfully. Looking pastward
is no sin; living backwards likely is.

A Memory of Time

It is only habit and memory
that dulls the physical passion*, not time.
If time were the culprit, we would not find
ourselves missing in action as we have.
Nor is it memory, for I recall
the touch of your hands, my dear, the kisses
sweet and slow, tasting of one another.
Our memories would serve much better—
would help us to find moments we could be
together, forgetting others exist.
No, it is indeed habit, the routines
of everyday existence, dulling us
to desire, breaking down the passion
waiting to remember just the right time.

*from Einstein's Dreams, by Alan Lightman

LANDMARKS

Did a time exist we didn't know each
other? My memories lie and tell me
there never was; this lie is one I like,
and so let it pass. We know each other
now, and our flame is bright enough to dim
the stars on new-moon nights, or shed the gray
any overcast day. It can only
be like this because of yesterdays that
taught us how to love and what to value
most and least—things material or not,
things of heart or soul or flesh, or something
that mingles all in some holistic way.
It is life's road and what turns we took that
got us this far—where we are together.

το Bε τhε Book

Oh to be the words scattered across the
pages, capturing your undivided
attention—or the pages caressed with
each stroke of your finger as you turn them.
Better yet, would that I were but the book
itself, a cherished place beside your bed
cradled by your hands into the late hours
of evening; resting on your chest when you
at last close your eyes, falling into dream.
Yes, I would be the names of those places—
and people—far from this reality
that grace the well worn tombs you burrow in,
Igniting in your imagination
a world apart from where we are today.

LONGER LOVED

If I had become an evangelist
like I once thought I would, then, love, would you
have reason to wish yourself that precious
tome for which I would sacrifice so much
without regard for your needs or desires,
putting that good book and holiness first
and above worldly things and flesh demands.
But I chose to be a lowly poet,
and so all my time and sacrifice
is spent among many books and pages,
seeking a different salvation than that
offered by suspicious scriptures and strict,
iron morality. Written pages
are momentary, you are longer loved.

nowhere so far away

The distance between us is only as
far as our thoughts, but how far thoughts travel!
Strange to think of these spaces as distance,
when the thought of you is beyond the curve
of my mind. Nevertheless, somewhere in
the cavernous reaches of my mind (I
am certain it's one inch right of center)
you uphold the torch that brightens my way.
Nowhere is so far away as beside
me when my mind has wandered away from
thoughts of you. Know, dear, that I am never
too far to hear your voice call out to me.
No matter. Here you are, and now too dear
to wander from. I keep you safe from fear.

REALITY'S WESTERN EDGE

Though the sun shines outside, I am stuck here
in this dismal basement, manacled
to a corner workstation—and how not-
ergonomical it is at that! Here,
imagination is the only link
to sanity, and daydream the only
panacea for workday fevers that
rage through us creative souls never meant
for such regimentation. We escape
only through creative expression acts.
I am with you and your elves in faerie
fields on reality's western edge, where
the sun rises eight hours every day,
then sets eight hours, till starlit moonrise.

ΤΟ ΟCCUPY ΤΙΜΕ

To occupy time while you're gone, I work
nothing too urgent—just things here and there
I want to do to keep my mind busy,
odds and ends—projects much larger than I
thought they would be. Secret surprises, love,
something to bring a smile to your face
when you walk into our home, missing me
as I miss you. I try to concentrate
on images of what I want to do
with you when you return. Memories come
with the scent of your pillow in my arms.
I long for you and realize I am
incomplete, though enough to be myself
so I occupy time waiting for you.

VIRTUE'S DAUGHTER

Who'd have thought we would be good examples
for others in love? Kissing and cooing
wherever the impulse grabs us, groping
each other without concern for spying
eyes or jealous glares, with outright contempt
for stilted prudes and other shame-mongers
who would stifle all such public displays
and spread their heretical ideas
about abstinence as true purity,
and coitus as original sin, when
we know better. Sincere affection is
life's greatest virtue—and love its daughter.
Writing sonnets, kissing often, loving
well—that is our example to the world.

OUR OWN EXISTENCE

I catch the look of the other women—and
some of the men too—who sit in the crowd,
listen to the words read at microphone
and whispered among tables, I see them
they smirk or smile or sneer when I touch you,
the edge of your sleeve, my fingers along
the back of your neck and kiss you. Should I
withdraw my hand? Refrain from reaching out
to touch he who is mine to love, honor,
and cherish simply because they find it
upsetting? No, I will not pull away
from expressions of our love—let them learn
to live with love and enjoy—as we do
with words, laughter, and our own existence.

chALLENGES

Some nights, sleep is illusive, and when it
comes it brings disturbing dreams. On those nights,
our mutual presence seems so much more
important, whether dreams be yours or mine;
and to awaken with a warm shoulder
and supportive kisses is the only
escape from nightmare. Such is tenderness
we share, that it brings solace such mornings.
So many the lines we scrawl of dreamlands
we walk in softer light, but nightmares come
and peace only bears in reality's
shadowed substance. Such is the real world.
Hell, high waters, and disconcerting dreams
are just challenges we face together.

PEACE COMES

In the shadowed hours before we wake
demons enter my dreams, fears chase away
all your sunlight whispered words of love.
And I struggle to wake within your arms
shoulders tied in knots while I slept beside
you. I cannot explain my dreams except
in their threats against our life together.
I feel for your warmth—and touch the darkness.
Restless, you toss and turn in your sleep, too,
saddled to some nightmare, caught up inside
your own battle. Waking finds you twisted,
sleep deprived, groggily searching my kiss.
Reaching daylight once again, peace comes and
rubs sore muscles with relaxing whispers.

MyCHS OF SEPARATION

Sometimes I have nothing to say to you
because words are empty of what I would
could I say what you should hear of feelings
that grow from your words and evident strain
over things that remain unchangeable
since Pandora first loosed them from her box.
Prime victim of patriarchal envy—
Matriarch of all us troubled humans
bereft of 'Grace'—Paradise's evicts,
doomed to live fallen lives in fallen worlds;
and though Hephaestus may reject us,
we have fused as few separate selves have.
On one call's wings our history pivots,
Chalk one up to sweet Serendipity!

BOUNCE

Bounced back from beyond the edge of who knows
where—that place you find yourself when the world
gives you more than you know you can handle—
and I landed in your lap. You, too, on
the bounce around, wondering where to land,
you were caught unawares, like a deer in
the headlights. Blinded by the past, we fell
tumbling together into today
and now we're dreaming of our tomorrows
never apart. I would not trade my pain
for any of the times we have shared since
meeting in the emptiness of cyber
space and one phone call later life changed to
a place I knew I could live forever.

i AM COLD

I am cold—colder still beneath these sheets
rain pelted windows reflect once-full moon
light now slowly fading in the winter
night's sky. I can enjoy the rain with you
but alone I feel insignificant.
The warmth of you—your body, breath, and life—
is missing and I am missing you, love.
These nights apart tell me what I knew yet
refused to believe. I don't like being
by myself any more. Those days are gone.
Oh, I don't mind an hour or two but
cannot handle nights with nothing to hold
but pillows scented with your essence and
the impression of where you lay your head.

Love's essence

Yes. How cold these sheets sans either other.
Rain is but a tapping melancholy
thing when one misses other gone away,
but warmth lies in knowing our reunion
is but a little away! Oh, but how
long a day for lovers separated
who know both joy and sorrow in loving,
having lost in life and love long before
winning as have you and I! And tempered
though we are by life's pressured heat and love,
no panacea shall ever fully
cure hearts so open, neither from sorrow
nor from infrequent lonely hours apart.
This is our love's essence: patient knowledge.

SCATTER PAGES

Scattered about the house, remnants of us,
our thoughts, can be found on half-used notebooks.
Words we penned to begin a tale, poem,
or letter to loved ones, sit unfinished
waiting for our return. But we rarely
go back to where we were. Always moving
forward—trying to stem the flow of back-
ward motion into the past we would
just as soon forget. Those missives become
less important as the moment we first
wrote the words disappears. Yesterday is
meant to stay as a place of memories.
We glance at pages half-written and see
our present is full of our life and love.

MiLe MARKeRS

Pages half-filled with our thoughts are not yet
remnants, as we are still here to claim them.
Our space is cluttered with signs of life lived
well and free of fastidiousness as
regards tidiness. Our house is cleaner
for being less tidy because it shines
mutual light from complementing souls
who share so openly. How dull to hide
all this passion and thought within some dark
drawer or hang it in disused file folders
where we'd likely never pick it up again.
Yesterday is today's road behind us,
whence we came to converge into this now—
memories but mile-markers we've passed by.

WHEN ALONE

Shadows dance down passages beside me
keeping time in poem and rhyme, memory
written in a language I know but don't
remember hearing before you and I—
a time you spoke of love to another
I become tangled in this thought-picture
inside those words—someone else reading them
out loud to you, asking her own questions
I search for any note of our promise
in your words back to her—yet hear nothing
Echoes of the past evaporate in
the existence of now—your love and mine
in tangled emotions caught up in time
surviving in spite of scared memories.

THEN, NOW AND TOMORROW

I am no more the man who wrote those poems
than you are the woman to whom I wrote
before I knew you. She exists no more
as that woman, either—whoever she
then was. Do you fear some echo years hence
of yourself reading poems present, haunted
again by poets past? Perish the thought!
What purpose in envy of what is not?
Content you in that which now is—my love—
and promise for tomorrow, not spoken
but written in language more permanent
than mere breath or ink have power to scribe,
much less enforce. Our promise resides in
Nature's truths—unassuageable ethos.

BURIED IN STORY

I lay on my side on a soft pillow
of water, watch as you peck away words
a distraction from surgical daylight.
Stories weave themselves around your fingers
tangled in the present tense of our lives.

I see you miss our boys, hear you key stroke
their futures in fantasy, dreams once held
perhaps for you in younger existence
keeps you busy creating another
place and time where this fear doesn't invade.

Whispers escape my lips soundless to you
Lose yourself this night buried in story
and when you've exhausted your mind enough
come lay with me atop this soft cushion.

YOUR FATHER'S DAUGHTER

Omission is your lie—absent all spite,
meaning only quiet answer for fears
that threaten to unhinge a delicate
balance where you dance the fence between
Reason and Hell; and it's too often you
pirouette closer to its burning side
though never by deliberate stance / step.
I gaze in wonder at your stubborn grace,
your father's daughter heart-wide, marrow-deep
you refuse gravity's demand to fall—
decline your own body's harsh insistence
to succumb to Death's summons even for
waking's brief demise of nightly repose—
You push through, with me ever at your side.

Life Dwells Within Our Lines

My writing is not purposed to escape
either the horror of coming cutting
or dread of your collapse from worried night's
waiting. It has not eluded my full
attention that tomorrow your father,
now also mine in law and affection,
will be opened like a book, edited
for malign syntax, censored for content,
and bound again with meaner stitches than
his original publisher's. Neither
has it escaped my heart to worry, dear,
that death prowls too close these precious persons
and by so doing threatens our own lives
with tragic change. I write to affirm life.

WHAT STORMS MAY COME

I'm lost. If I could find another way
to survive, to get through this, then I would—
perhaps from a distance would be better,
as long as you are together with me.
I cringe every time I think about it.
Anger and impatience overwhelm me.
Frustration, a beast rabid for my soul
holds me prisoner in my emotions.
Your love sweet soft anchor that holds me fast.
Without you real, I drift weightless dreamlike
out past shallow, falling toward the water
tumbling out in to insanity.
Hold to my hand ever, keep me safe warm
help me weather this storm as I help you.

public displays

Sweet-breathed lovers see in glances, double
mint kisses, and stolen moments, pleasures
some find immoral in public display.
Unwilling to hide beneath the cover
of night or behind closed doors, we open
other eyes to the possibility
of renewing love and vows many times
over as each day awakens passion's
affirmations—bright-eyed laughter spoken
in tenderness with words of beauty, soft
intimacies meant for nobody else.
Through silver gifts and fine-tipped fountain pens
our words recreate magic in tune with
the waxing and waning of love complete.

IRONY OF BRANDING

It's a fine thing to see affections spent
in public displays when not pretentious.
Funny how society finds it more
forgiving to exhibit violence
and hatred—that profane gestures and foul
verbiage elicit fewer and lesser
criticisms than a pat on the ass,
or even a chaste kiss sans tongue—forbid
it that there should be true passion flaunted
where virgin eyes might see and be soiled.
But you were made for loving me, baby;
And I was made for loving you. We can't
be held apart by those flinted gazes
or envy of iron men who'd brand us.

pLAY AT SOLiTAiRE

wrap tightly around the space between us
when you can't step inside and wait with me
for frustration's intrusion to pass by
too many distractions pulling at time
stretching it thinly across the moments
meant to be ours alone—or together
minutes we were to spend remembering
our first kiss, the touch that took forever
a second before we two connected.
realize without remorse that my love
is patient, unwavering, ever yours
play at solitaire knowing I am near
filling physical space or as shadow
in the corner, always close by my love.

Distances

Times it seems nothing separates us two
from solitary oneness. Whether miles
or millimeters intervene between
your flesh and mine, we touch one another
sans contact—a deeper understanding
of true marriage through one casual glance
than could issue from a thousand kisses;
yet so much depends upon those kisses
and flirtations throughout days, nights, years . . .
Touching goes beyond skin to skin within
our life of love, yet it visits there, too,
often as we feel touchy-feely, feel
like feeling outside what inside keeps us
close within distances both far and near.

ҒAUX POSITIVE

Some days I can't even hold on to the few
words I've left in my brain. Fingers won't work.
Mind wanders aimlessly around, casting
about for something to bring to focus.

More often than not, lately, I come up
empty. Too many things to think about,
too little time for me to figure out
where I am, wish I was, or "ought" to be.

All test results are negative which is
positive, except it doesn't tell me
why I feel as I do, so I begin
to believe that I must be mad or worse—

I could be human after all . . . I guess
perhaps the problem all along was stress.

UNDER A HEAVY LOAD

Months now, I have watched straws accumulate,
wondering if the next makes you broken-
backed camel, or whether you'll finally
learn to unpack your luggage and resist
loads others unintentionally toss
on your overload. It is comical
in a most tragic way to see someone
undertake such Herculean labors
in atonement for imagined shortfalls
and guilts better owned by others. But you
bunch your shoulders in Atlas-like poses
and let us pile it on as though you were
that titan and equal to a struggle
in which you are less alone than you feel.

MAN IN THE BLACK FEDORA

Leaning against the corner he watches
from beneath the tilt of a faded black
fedora—his trademark stance, his blue eyes
narrow as he follows the ladies with
long legs, grimacing at the height of their
stiletto heels. Memories of painful

encounters with just those shoes run across
his mind. To shake them loose he grabs a pack,
slides out an unfiltered camel, and lights
himself another step closer to death.
It don't matter to anyone—except
her—his lady love. He calls her green-eyes

cause he thinks she's got a thing about him
and the past—though she knows what's done is done.

visiting hours

What's done is done she tells him. But it lies
in her eyes to wonder how history
repeats and whether they play the same roles
though characters have changed. His cigarette
won't tell him truth, nor smoke screen images
conjured from recollection. They must know
that faith is believing past the knowledge
of what seems to what can be reality.

She's traded in high-heels for sensible
shoes; he smokes fewer filters now in hope
of living longer to extend their love—
secure a future they build by the day.
The past is a great place to visit—
but who the hell wants to live there?

PORTENT

I'd like to pull out my eyes, scratch behind
the emptiness, rid myself of this pain,
the itch of tears threatening. I cannot
think or read or write my way out – away
from this place. On my walk in the morning
I wonder at the red tail's arrival
Is he some portent? Of good? Of evil?
Or sorrow waiting on the front door steps
lingering like an illness nobody
wants to acknowledge as it eats away
at fragile happiness, cultivated
over the years to spite the naysayers.

There yesterday, again today, my hawk—
I will see you as a sign to be strong.

TOTEM

His flight arrested, the hawk takes his post
to signal you—never alone—watching
is his thing, take his contentment to heart
and know he watches over all of us.

How ignorant we are of what we host
in our hearts—fear—tiny demons lunching
on our souls and cells, tearing all apart
dreams and hopes and loves, passions that make us.

How alone you are is no question—no,
the question is how alone feel and think:
our totems tell us alone is nonsense;
solitude is myth, one we seldom grow
weary of retelling though it might sink
us. Hawk is your totem, your good defense.

WHEN LONELY SITS LARGE

My place in life is not at the center
of anyone's but my own, no matter
how I look at it—or think I want you
to see me on days when lonely sits large,
blocks my view of the world outside my place.

Our lives, full of coming and going, want
for nothing beyond boundaries we set
which, when all is said, are as limitless
as our imaginations, spanning space
and time together, both leading our lives

separately, yet always with the other
tucked deep inside, cradled next to the heart.
So I remind myself, my place exists
in our lives together and separately.

TOGETHERNESS OF DISTANCES

Far too long since I penned you a sonnet;
I hear your silent cry, see it in lines
though my mind seems hawk-distant, and my heart
lies dusty in a drawer with no business . . .
Am I so far away from you? Am I
a galaxy distant despite skin on skin?
My sin—I repent me now—forgive me?
Our journey together staggers lately
in ruts of mishap and blue circumstance,
but skies shine on, we shine on . . . these cloudy
days but a passing of real-time Doppler
on screens that merely represent the real.
We are together in the realest sense,
commitment: a togetherness of distance.

SHADES OF ONE ANOTHER

Where I am today I see life growing
together with life, the fabric of me
weaving with yours, spinning our memories
beyond imaginations' here and now.

Grey pinstripes, lavender, brings out blue sparks
covers your body while I undress you
with my eyes—in my mind—when we're alone,
in a stranger's crowd or among friends.

Comfortable in matching Jimmy Buffet
blue palm trees or Chinese good luck coins.
Jeans and a freshly pressed tee cling closely
as do our bodies wrapped 'round each other.

We are black and white, bare flesh, all colors
blended into shades of one another.

UPWARD MOBILITY

So much lonely in your voice some mornings,
husband too sleepy-eyed, you walk the dog
alone—it resonates throughout your day
through the phone, sounds of ominous warnings . . .

Depression's not your style, though you do bog
down with worry sometimes, how well delay
storms with a sunny outlook, carry on
as though no stone may bruise the heel of one

always moving up steeper mountainsides
constantly on the go, never upon
peaks to stand, rungs in Jacob's ladder—sun
and moon and stars but heaven's firesides—

but no, we know when to still our striving,
rest awhile, sate on love, keep reviving.

MORNING RITUAL

Whipped egg-white clouds scatter themselves across
the morning sky, shattering the blue hue
with piles of froth, dark along their bottoms,
signaling storms ready to thunder through.

Behind cranberry curtains you sprawled out
beneath our covers. Your body relaxed
face free of lines, full of sleep and dreaming
I almost hate to wake you, so I pause—

watch a moment as memory blushes
my cheeks, warms my body, the desire
to run away with you overwhelms me.
Unable to resist, I stroke your cheek,

whisper my request and you turn, hand out
and so our morning ritual begins.

BETWEEN THE DEW - DAYBREAK

This walk through cloud-tear threads strung across
fields in early morning's peaceful quiet
provides a start to the chaotic day,
allows me to see what waits just beyond
the possibilities of my present.

Last night's tossing turns from lethargy to
energy in early daylight's cool breezes
softer than a lover's kisses, eyes closed
I make love to the sunrise images:
your sleeping form beneath covers, naked . . .

somewhere in between the dew and daybreak
I find you in my dreams—even when awake.

DEW AT DAYBREAK

Not even six o'clock and it's nearly
ninety—if you count the heat index. But
it's a humid heat . . . Why is it that we
take snow days in winter, but not heat days
when God Himself lounges in cooler shade?
No sense borrowing trouble, we walk the dog
from habit and necessity—our health
and his—and to strengthen relationships.
I doubt he's concerned with the latter, though,
as it is manifestly human to
worry over such abstractions. Okay
for him to take for granted his place here—
let's take a lesson from the sitting brute,
sit in dew-jeweled grass, live, love and pant.

MORNING (WITHOUT) MOURNING

Eyes grow heavy with sleep against my will,
I would stay awake to watch you read through
night hours, your attention divided
between book and football always close by
yet somewhere else beside me as I sleep.

Morning darkness now, no light to walk by
and still I wake and rise to walk the dog,
wishing with all my might I could return
to sleep more hours away, wake with you
and wander through the day in lighter mood.

Foolish to fill my morning with mourning,
for those few hours we're apart, it's dark.
I greet the day without you by my side
yet carry you with me through every stride.

TOO INDEBTED

Foolish, you claim, to spend morning mourning,
and yet your debt of worry weighs our days—
karma calls to collect, we borrow more
and drive our nerves into the red . . . Weary,
why wonder what weighs us into worthless
weeks of depression? Anxiety costs
more than "household expenses"—I wonder
how high interest is on such deficits.
Let's stop. Let's pay it forward in laughter,
declare ourselves bankrupt of sorrow, give
up maudlin mornings for a shining rise,
and smile our way into kinder karma.
Our vows are set. Our choice now is simply
how to go about living "for better."

A PARTNER FOR THIS JOURNEY

You make the house we live in home simply
by being there. I look around at all
the clutter, see piles of paper, pictures,
and reminders of your presence mingled

with mine. And I don't see a mess, rather
a place where you are comfortable to be
you and I, me; where laughter and tears are
exchanged in the every day where we love.

I find I no longer seek the castle
with its high walls and prince on his white horse.
Real life is much more than the dreams I had
as a girl of twenty or thirty years.

Together with you I have found it all
plus a partner for this journey through life.

NEVER REACH OUT

That's what they warned us, "never reach out to
save one from falling." Lest they pull you too
down with them in century-long tumbles
off words' ends. What rusty knight fumbles
in dragons' lairs? Hang their jaded prudence!
Daring consequence defines chivalry
and champions defy with impudence
all hell's imposture and dark deviltry
for glories' sake and salvations' advent.
But love makes heroes of us all—and fools
lose the day to locked hearts. Our love's ascent
shows the world below our precipice, cools
us with tempered mountain breeze, shows our route
clearly. Neither to fall, neither reach out.

wheN i AM uN-weLL

Shadows beneath my eyes, under over
cast skies the weather colors my mood, dark
don't see clearly—can't hear words being said
muffled as they are through layers of fog.

Insecurity blanket wrapped tightly
I watch you watch the world go by beyond
reach. The view from two tables away fills
your mind's eye, images blend together.

Reach out, grab a hold of my hand, shake me.
Pull me out of this cocoon covering.
Peel back the layer that separates us,
show me tenderness, passion all for me

alone. I sit waiting without asking
to be shown and told—in one breathless kiss.

CENTER ME

You're my angel in a sky of Black—star
of only twinkle in chaos; steadfast
in this brute perpetual rotation
ratmaze treadmill of a year only you
have centered this
                          vertigo, still maelstrom
of demand and demand and cyclonic
burden of pay pay pay more do more do more
be better get it here on time early
earlier now yesterday it's past due
trouble and worry and pray to cease to
rest to repose give us respite oh heavens we are
so overwhelmed in spite of paving hell over
with cobbles of good intentions surfeit
and flood of deeds.
                          Oh, how you center me.

ssshhhh

Remember—silence is sometimes the best
answer to your unspoken questions. I
cannot always give you what you need to
survive—yet when I give you all of me,

I give you everything I have, the rest
is up to you. Ask me how, when or why—
I may just smile. Not knowing what to do
is okay—listen to the silence, see

what it has to say to you, perhaps test
your own time in quiet, give it a try
find your way to me as I do to you
in stillness, in between my dreams where we

speak unspoken thoughts, hear our own laughter.
Remember silence can be the answer.

RApt By YOU

There are times your penchant for borrowing
trouble echoes through me in resonance
to the past. "Waiting for the other shoe
to drop"—or not to drop. And what a shoe!
But imagination is better used
in pursuits other than creating grief.
You taught me that. We learned it together
better than most I've seen. And yet we have
this insidious habit of downturns. . .
It is nights like this when we surprise each
other that turn out the silver linings—
getting fresh like teenagers and necking
on the couch, coy and giggling and later
we ravish each other like newlyweds.

WRAPPED IN YOU

I have difficulty remembering
when it was other than you and me and
yet I clearly see and feel the remnants
of those past relationships when I wake
with a start from nightmares that haven't left.

I reach out for comfort in your skin pressed
close to my own, soft breath sounds audible
beneath the blankets piled to keep us warm.
I count on my fingers how many years
we have been an "us" and I am in awe.

Four years feels forty seconds, minutes, years
and in the blink of an eye, here we are
four and half years from that first moment
when I knew my life would be wrapped in you.

Life Before You

On days I let myself wander along
memories of life before we two met,
some scenes are beautiful yet still empty
of the light surrounding me now you're here.

I cannot deny there were wondrous
moments in my life. Long years ago now,
when others crowded the corners, I
lived to please everyone, saving myself

for last. Yet now, past those memories I
have, are new images—dreams come alive.
And a glance back past all the ups and downs
makes years between then and now seem so short

yet then again, I wonder if a time
exists when we did not know each other.

chis WONOERFUL Life

I, too, recall empty scenes previous
to our recognition, our union, our
revelation of wholeness in each other.
I remember how I loved solitude
so much that I hated people, how you
showed me the bright beauty of tolerance
and the violet comfort of company
in a house where voices raise for joyous
occasion—where red anger is dealt with
in logic's lavender tones to heal us
and edify our humanity with
reason and the commitment to nurture
each other in important matters, to
save each other from life's river of strife.

The Best Truth

Never so well expressed in words was what
your eyes, your own particular tilt
of chin, wrote in flesh and charged air between
here and there, where you gaze at me—at what
your heart, silent, testifies; its lilt
of breathless inarticulate, serene
emotion speaks to mine through open eyes
to a heart receptive to your wordless
conversations and speechless eulogies.
For poets to write of words' weakness flies
in the face and spirit of Parnassus—
but Truth is higher and better to please.

Silence sometimes is the best truth to tell,
cliché, other times, apropos as well.

OVER-SIZED SHIRT

I feel sexy in this over-sized shirt
with the button-down collar so proper.
No tie around my neck and the buttons
all undone, it hangs loosely down to my

thighs—not reaching my knees. With it I wear
ankle socks, no shoes—or anything else.
For fun I brush my hair, tousling it
for the rumpled look and pout at myself

in the mirror. I smile knowing you would
wink at me, and whistle—were you to walk
in and find me playing dress-up with your
white shirt. It smells like you and I cannot

bring myself to wash away the scent—you
hold me when I wear this over-sized shirt.

YOUR PERFECT ACCESSORY

I never got the game of dress-up, unless
you count a few Halloweens, interviews
for jobs I didn't want, and posing as
a poet of archaic ages. You
pose and play less than you used to—and not
because you've grown up so much as you have
to be the grown-up these days. Look at me—
frowns and all too serious! Frightening
clown, me. I should play more with you; we should
dance more. Somewhere deep within, I notice
and giggle with delight every time I
see you pirouette from stove to sink. You
become pure light, lavender rose, in those
moments. Joy—your perfect accessory!

sweet delight

My lips wrap around this sweet confection
a gift from you—my love—a delicious
reminder of your desire for me
to be happy and have treats that are mine

alone—not shared by others in our house.
I smile at the creamy richness of this
candy, my mouth alive with memories
of the taste of you, no subtle flavor

our love-making. It is bold and honest,
passion blended with such soft caresses
I weep at the thought and laugh with delight
as this gift of sugary affection

brings you closer to me across the miles
that separate our separate beds tonight.

MY LOVELY (CHOCOLATE VENDOR)

You spoil me shamelessly. No new news there—
our friends, neighbors, kids all know. I think our
dog may even understand that he's not
the most spoiled kid in the house—though
at my age, a lack of maturation
applies more than anything. It's your bad
habit to supply my bad habits. Some
would call ours a codependent lifestyle,
but I'm happy to recognize my great
addiction to chocolates and other
sweets. Funny how I would never purchase
them for myself, but they taste so divine
given from your hand. . . I'm certain hemlock
would turn to my ambrosia if you poured.

i REMAINED QUIET

This morning, as I lay beside you in
the fading darkness, I wanted you, love.
The warmth of your body pressed against mine,
your hand resting on my breast, brought curls of

heat spiraling up through me. Your stillness,
the steady rhythm of your breathing, stopped
me. I have this passion growing inside,
quenchable only by a kiss from you,

a touch of your hand, a look that says you
have eyes for me alone. I let you sleep,
not wanting to rob you of precious rest.
So, instead of reaching to touch—caress—

I remained quiet, listened to you breathe—
the sound of love echoing in our room.

ECHOES OF OUR BREATH

Seems too often we stand watches, one sleeps
while the other lays awake in worry
about the day, the night, the bills—what keeps
us awake seems to change with the hurry
of harried lives. One day this, the next night
another concern—health, wealth, or the lack
of this or that. It lurks, waits to attack
under cover of darkness and gaslight.
We sleepless linger, yet something there is
that takes rest from quiet insomnia
despite unsettled thoughts—something there is
that finds simple pleasure, if not euphoria,
in echoes of the other's breath off these walls
of our mutual life. Love's echo calls.

NAKED OF INHIBITION

Sweat trickles down between my breasts and you
tell me I'm beautiful in the day's heat
fresh from mowing the lawn or garden work
my cheeks so flushed, and sun-blessed hair a mess—

your words caress me, cool breeze kisses sweet
momentarily quenching the deep thirst
only to leave me hungry for more, love.
One or two more strokes to peak my desire.

Overheated flesh burns beneath your gaze
I am stripped naked of inhibition
starved for a taste of you and unashamed
as I blossom in this new life with you.

I am young in mind and body, spirit
joined with yours—whole and alone, together.

AWAKING INTO DREAMS

Reality, they say, is subjective,
and you are my subject in ours. We think
dreams lack substance, or at least some teach so,
and that what our minds create is less real
than those concrete bastions of tangible
experience. Yet how less real this, our
sharing of spirit we call love, than that
memory they consent to designate
as material reality? We
should burn their bastions! Set fire to their
falsehoods—grab life by its . . . carpe diem,
and realize that lucid dreaming is
our high redoubt, our bold engineering
of love and life as our souls blueprint it.

4 1/2 OR 55

Eyes open wide, these images show me
my desire for you doesn't cool with time
or distance. Pictures painted from memory
create fantasies new—real and sublime.

Sensations and visual cues taken
from secret corners, where I hide away
all my wildest dreams—those rarely shaken
loose—surface and find their place on display,

easily read in the smile that graces
full lips ready for my lover's kisses.
I whisper words to explain the places
to touch, exactly with no near misses.

If four and a half years or fifty-five,
you fill my world—keep fantasies alive.

TREASURES

Eyes wide open or tight closed, dreams linger
beyond states of sleep or half-waking; we
hold them, treasures greater than gold and gems.
Years are merely markers, freeze-frames of life's
epic film, and we are stars in every
scene. Our kisses light the silver screen, Slim
and Steve mere metaphors of us, passion
posed by a hundred stars. They envy us
the real life they live only in film hours
we live everyday in every day. Our
love no fiction any could believe, so
real, so true, even poets cower, their
figures and conceits stilled in mute awe
and each wonders jaded where paradise lost.

Leaky Ceilings

Full moon hidden by thunder clouds my brain
I want sleep but rise to check the ceiling
fearful of the drip drip drip of raindrops
electronics do not like the water.

If he wouldn't smell upon our return
I'd have taken the dog for a walk, pushed
you out of bed—with gentle reminders
of your promise to walk with us today.

But the ceiling was leaking, and the bath
called sweetly that it would welcome me in
subtle-scented water, a few minutes
of relaxation before the daybreak . . .

I love the rain—when it doesn't leak through
the ceiling and push me into the bath.

honey-do undone

Home owning is such hard work. Fourteen times
we've tarred the seam, and still it insists on
leaking when winds blow southeasterly down-
pours and overwhelms too gradual a grade;
this old house was not well planned. It was put
together in pieces—twice add-ons stuck
on like afterthoughts twice reconsidered,
and rushed sans blueprints. It was engineered
like our love—conceived in a passionate
moment and expanded as life grew with
it and around it. Love needs our constant
cultivation; perhaps the ceiling leaks
to water passion, gentle reminder
that even lasting things need nurturing.

i CAN WRITE

Ink wells parched—dust filled quill rests against curled
edges of parchment waiting for words blown
away in the darkness. Stars pin-prick night
restless waiting for words from you despite
my understanding that the wait will be
long and lonely. Our journey has staggered
but not fallen—this saves me from myself
keeps me from fumbling, stumbling in
to the blue mood of despair. I can write
lines to you in my dreams and between notes
in meetings meant to capture attention
intrigue and bring me closer to success
in a place I don't care about nearly
as much as I care about you and me.

YOU COLOR ME

From childhood I was razed to see black/white—
learning, for God's sake!, to judge wrong from right,
and call a spade a spade, to quote the Ten,
to, from rote, quote it-is-written scriptures.
Adulthood became a path to The Light,
my path through seminary to pulpits,
thumping Bibles and roaring hellfire, drunk
on some semblance of the Holy Spirit.
But sin crept up, my eyes opened to hues
of life our ministers warned us about—
and Truth opened my heart to the spectrum
of experience—How could Creation
be intended a bed of suffering?
Heaven sent you to color me living.

SiLLy whispeReD wORDs

Flip between screens, hidden poems unseen
by prying eyes that peer over shoulders
hunched against the chill of office windows.
I write the silly words of whispered love
still so unsure they have come together
the way I want—express the way I want
to hold you in my arms, kiss away frowns
too frequently found across your blue eyes,
humor harbored inside the harshness of
cynicism, the bark of a laugh aimed
at the outside world—time's cruelty bent
on pushing us into a sharp corner
where our only hope is to hang on to
each other, writing silly whispered words.

WORDS WHISPERED

Last night you whispered in your dream a name
I'd nearly forgotten. Sad at the thought,
I tossed and rolled for hours trying to
put it out of my head. Now's not the time—
There's much to do, my fictional refrain
comes from sublimated fact. But later
is long past due, and it's time we hashed out
a plan to resolve this issue again.
St. Genevieve! There, discussion open;
we need to find our way back to that old
B&B we first stayed in there. Now if
only you'd whisper that name in your dreams,
I could get to sleep, get rested, and quit
feeling like we never go anywhere.

the myth of security

So much of what we need we have. And yet
life teaches us too much to depend on
external powers to feed our gnawing
wants. Love, security—emotional
necessities—how often we seek them
outside ourselves! But they are not outside
us; they come from within. Our eyes and hearts
seem too often to search within others
for what we cannot see within ourselves—
And this is the power of love, that it
illuminates the me in you and you
within me so that we see what it is
we've searched so long to find, no external
thing, but the power of self-truth fulfilled.

chicken soup

Blacken one pound of chicken in garlic
and olive oil; boil one gallon water
with bullion and half bulb of garlic;
put chicken in boiling water (save juice
with garlic); brown one pound chicken, peppered
to taste, and put in soup (save juice); sear third
pound of chicken, put in simmering pot.
Let soup simmer on low for one to three
hours. Add pasta noodles (experiment
with types: farfalla, elbow, bowtie or
linguini). Boil to taste (al denté works
best for starters—pasta softens with each
reheating). Add more garlic to extreme
of taste—and love makes it a panacea.

in sickness and in health

With blankets tucked in close around my feet
I watch you putter about, fix supper,
stoop to scratch the dog's ear, everyday things
missed in the hustle and bustle when well.

Grilled Muenster and chicken soup, homemade good
to ease the ache of flu and fear and stress.
Bite-sized bits between spoon-slurps and sniffles.
You take care of me, warm the chills away.

Asleep, your hand resting on my belly
protective heat to ward off night terrors
those dreams turned in to horror scenes of death
for lack of oxygen, you breathe for me.

Smiles exchanged across the room, remind us
—in sickness and in health, for life—longer.

IN ABSENCE AND IN PRESENCE

Each day worth having? Even those I'm mad
as a hatter—and angry as the devil?
Some mornings don't shine, my soul too distant
to capture starlight. Yet you penetrate
darkness abysses I cannot begin
to comprehend, let alone articulate.
A stroke of your hand, one smile from your eyes
and hell sheds from me like a snake's molting—
then you leave, and I know heaven's rejected
me for the duration of your absence. How
could I have conned you into this? Marriage
on the best of days is never stronger
than it has to be on these worst of days.
Yet better and worse, we are together.

ONCE UPON A PROPOSAL

No one knelt down and held a hand in theirs.
Candlelight did not flicker with love's flame.
Memories of a spring morning came to mind.
Trouble and turbulence melted away—
insignificant as our life began.

Whispers from behind the hands of others
questioned the wisdom of too-soon nuptials—
they could not see through jaded eyes, the love
two people found when their souls collided
each in just the right place at the right time.

Mastery of marriage, a task not lightly
taken on by even the bravest of
beings, provides me with challenges still
yet each day is worth the having—with you.

Giddy

Funny how after years together we
ignore the oddities—a snore-filled night
unwashed hair for three days and circular
discussions. I can pull the covers up
over my ears and close my eyes—you are
as I first saw you—I see you every
time I look your way—handsome in my eyes.

Too frequently frowning or distracted
on Sunday afternoons meant more for games
an old movie, or book—rapt on the couch
your blues eyes manage an occasional
twinkle in my direction, and we laugh
even after so many ups and downs
I am still giddy at the thought of you.

serious business

A year gone by since you claimed giddiness,
and just now I reply—what a year! Dark
with overcast, heavy with burdens, cares
weighing down: debts, overdue bills, parking
tickets and taxes unexpectedly
come due in a lean month . . . More cares than you
can twinkle your giddy eyes at. Your stern
frown overshadows, fear clouds your once-clear
peridot eyes. They sparkle, though far less
often than those earlier years. But life
is serious business. Sometimes storms crash
against our shores and wreck a day or two.
Yet the sun soon or later returns to
warm us, wrapped in each other's arms and heart.

BREAKFAST IN A FOUR-POSTER

What words I whisper worries me—Paris?
Or some other lover long gone from dreams
relegated to nightmares I may scream
in whispered words when deep in sleep. Hold me,
push back fears that in daylight I can't speak.

Or maybe I am living in my dreams
practical matters left in frustration
from a week of ring-around-the-rosy
work and home never getting it all done—
laundry piles high like papers on my desk.

I do dream sweeter dreams—St. Genevieve
an escape, memories of a hot tub
and champagne, breakfast in a four-poster
renewing our vows, our lives, and our selves.

FRAGILE EMBRACE

Edge of angry creeps along consciousness
prepared for the inevitable all
while knowing it'll never arrive—yet
certain anyway it exists inside

debilitating—aggravating—stress
induced self-consciousness, that same old fear
my automatic negative thoughts grind
against one another—rub up against

life I know, feel, sense, even when alone
unfair—to me—to him—a memory
still lurks, biding its time, hunting me
when fragility embraces me close

hormones leak from the radio lyrics
rip me apart—hold me together—still